DEATHS DUELL

PLATE I

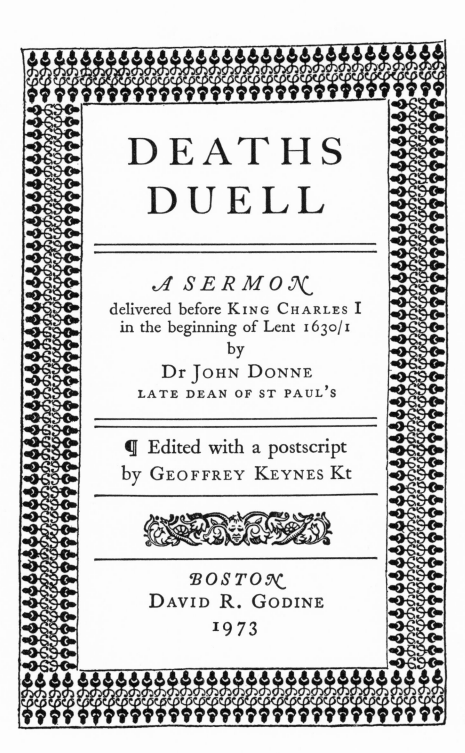

DEATHS DUELL

A SERMON
delivered before KING CHARLES I
in the beginning of Lent 1630/1
by
Dr JOHN DONNE
LATE DEAN OF ST PAUL'S

¶ Edited with a postscript
by GEOFFREY KEYNES Kt

BOSTON
DAVID R. GODINE
1973

Trade edition   ISBN: 0 87923 050 9
Deluxe edition   ISBN: 0 87923 051 7

Library of Congress Catalogue Card number: 72-75133

PRINTED IN GREAT BRITAIN

CONTENTS

ILLUSTRATIONS

DEATHS DUELL

OR

A CONSOLATION TO THE SOULE
AGAINST THE
DYING LIFE AND LIVING DEATH OF THE BODY

delivered in a sermon at Whitehall before the King's Majesty
in the beginning of Lent 1630

And unto God the Lord belong the issues of death (from Death)
PSA. 68. 20

UILDINGS stand by the benefit of their foundations that sustain them, support them; and of their buttresses that comprehend them, embrace them; and of their contignations that knit and unite them. The foundation suffers them not to sink; the buttresses suffer them not to swerve; the contignation and knitting, suffer them not to cleave. The body of our building is in the former part of this verse; it is this; *He that is our God, is the God of salvation; ad salutes,* of salvations in the plural, so it is in the original; the God that gives us spiritual and temporal salvation too. But of this building, the foundation, the buttresses, the contignation are in this part of the verse, which constitutes our text, and in the three diverse acceptations of the words amongst our expositors, *Unto God the Lord belong the issues of death.* For, first the foundation of this building,(that our God is the God of all salvations) is laid in this, *That unto this God the Lord belong the issues of death*; that is, it is in his

I

power to give us an issue and deliverance, even then when we are brought to the jaws and teeth of death, and to the lips of that whirl-pool, the grave; and so in this acceptation, this *exitus mortis*, this issue of death is *liberatio a morte*, a deliverance from death; & this is the most obvious, and most ordinary acceptation of these words, and that upon which, our translation laies hold, *The issues from death*. And then, Secondly, the buttresses, that comprehend and settle this building; that *He that is our God is the God of salvation* are thus raised; *Unto God the Lord belong the issues of death*, that is, the disposition and manner of our death, what kind of issue, and transmigration we shall have out of this world, whether prepared or sodain, whether violent or natural, whether in our perfect senses, or shak'd and disordered by sickness; there is no condemnation to be argued out of that, no judgment to be

[Psa. 116. 15] made upon that, for howsoever they dye; *precious in his sight, is the death of his Saints*, and with him are the issues of death, the ways of our departing out of this life, are in his hands; and so, in this sense of the words, this *Exitus mortis*, the issue of death, is *liberatio in morte*, a deliverance in death; not that God will deliver us from dying, but that he will have a care of us in the hour of death, of what kind soever our passage be; and this sense, and acceptation of the words, the natural frame & contexture doth well and pregnantly administer unto us. And then lastly, the contignation and knitting of this building, that he that is our God, is the God of all salvations, consists in this, *Unto this God the Lord belong the issues of death*, that is, that this God the Lord having united and knit both natures in one, and being God, having also come into this world, in our flesh, he could have no other means to save us, he could have no other issue out of this world, nor return to his former glory, but by death. And so in this sense, this *exitus mortis*, the issue of death, is *liberatio per mortem*, a deliverance by death, by the death of this God our Lord, Christ Jesus; and this is St. *Augustines* acceptation of the words, and those many and great persons, that have adhered to him. In all these three lines then, we shall look upon these words; first, as the God of power, the Almighty Father, rescues his servants from the jaws of death; and then, as the God of mercy, the glorious Son, rescued us, by taking upon himself the issue of death; and then, (between these two,) as the God of comfort, the holy Ghost rescues us from all discomfort by his blessed impressions before hand, that what manner of death soever be ordained for us, yet this *exitus mortis*, shall be *introitus in vitam*, our issue in death, shall be an entrance into everlasting life. And these three considerations, our deliverance *a morte*, *in morte*, *per mortem*, from death, in death, and by death, will abundantly do all the offices of the foundation, of the buttresses, of the contignation of this our building, that *He that is our God, is the God of all salvation*, because *Unto this God the Lord belong the issues of death.*

FIRST then, we consider this *exitus mortis*, to be *liberatio a morte*; that with *God the Lord are the issues of death*, & therefore in all our deaths, and deadly calamities of this life, we may justly hope of a good issue from him; and all our periods and transitions in this life, are so many passages from death to death. Our very birth, and en-

First Part. *A morte.*

Exitus a morte uteri. trance into this life, is *exitus a morte*, an issue from death; for in our mothers womb, we are dead so, as that we do not know we live; not so much as we do in our sleep; neither is there any grave so close, or so putrid a prison, as the womb would be to us, if we stai'd in it beyond our time, or died there, before our time. In the grave the worms do not kil us: We breed and feed, and then kill those worms, which we our selves produc'd. In the womb the dead child kils the mother that conceiv'd it, and is a murderer, nay a Parricide, even after it is dead. And if we be not dead so in the womb, so, as that being dead, we kill her that gave us our first life, our life

Psa. 115. [5.] 6. of vegetation, yet we are dead so as *Davids* Idols are dead; in the womb, we have eyes and see not, ears and hear not. There in the womb we are fitted for works of darkness, all the while deprived of light; and there, in the womb, we are taught cruelty, by being fed with blood; and may be damned though we be never born. Of our very making in the womb,

Psa. 139. 14.
118. 23.
100. 3. *David* saies, *I am wonderfully and fearfully made*, and, *Such knowledge is too excellent for me*; for, *Even that this is the Lords doing, and it is wonderful in our eyes. Ipse fecit nos*, It is he that hath made us, and not we our selves, no, nor our

[Job] 10. 8. Parents neither. *Thy hands have made me, and fashioned me round about*, saies *Job*; and, (as the original word is) *Thou hast taken pains about me*; and yet saies he, *Thou doest destroy me*: though I be the master-piece of the greatest Master, (man is so) yet if thou do no more for me, if thou leave me where thou mad'st me, destruction will follow. The womb which should be the house of life, becomes death it self, if God leave us there. That which God threatens so often, the shutting of the womb, is not so heavy nor so discomfortable a curse, in the first as in the latter shutting; nor in the shutting of barrenness, as in the shutting of weakness, when Children are come to the birth, and there is not strength to bring forth. Esa. 37. 3.

It is the exaltation of misery, to fall from a near hope of happiness. And in that vehement imprecation the Prophet expresses the highth of Gods anger *Give them O Lord; what* Ose. 9. 14. *wilt thou give them? give them a mis-carrying womb.* Therefore as soon as we are men, (that is, inanimated, quickned in the womb) though we cannot our selves, our Parents have reason to say in our behalves, *Wretched man that he is, who* Ro. 7. 24. *shall deliver him from this body of death?* for, even the womb is a body of death, if there be no deliverer. It must be he that said to *Jeremy, Before I formed thee I knew thee, and before* [Jer.] 1.5. *thou camest out of the womb I sanctified thee.* We are not sure that there was no kind of ship nor boat to fish in, nor to pass by, till God prescribed *Noah* that absolute forme of the Ark; that word which the holy Ghost by *Moses,* uses for the Ark, Exo. 2. 3. is common to all kinds of boats, *Thebah*; and is the same word that *Moses* uses for the boat that he was exposed in, that his mother laid him in an Ark of bullrushes. But we are sure that *Eve* had no Midwife when she was delivered of *Cain*; therefore she might well say, *Possedi virum a Domino,* Gen. 4. 1. I have gotten a man from the Lord; wholly, intirely from the Lord: it is the Lord that hath enabled me to conceive, the Lord that infus'd a quickning soul into that conception, the Lord that brought into the world that which himself had quickned; without all this might *Eve* say, my body had been but the house of death, and *Domini Domini sunt exitus mortis,* To God the Lord belong the issues of death.

But then this *Exitus a morte*, is but *Introitus in mortem*, this issue, this deliverance from that death, the death of the womb, is an entrance, a delivering over to another death, the manifold deaths of this world. We have a winding sheet in our Mothers womb, which grows with us from our conception, and we come into the world wound up in that winding sheet; for we come to seek a grave. And as prisoners, discharged of actions, may lie for fees, so when the womb hath discharged us, yet we are bound to it by cords of flesh, by such a string, as that we cannot go thence, nor stay there. We celebrate our own funeral with cries, even at our birth, as though our threescore, and ten years of life were spent in our Mother's labor, and our Circle made up in the first point thereof. We beg one Baptism with another, a sacrament of tears; and we come into a world that lasts many ages, but we last not. *In domo patris,* (saies our blessed Saviour, speaking of heaven) *multæ mansiones*, there are many mansions, divers and durable; so that if a man cannot possess a martyrs house, (he hath shed no blood for Christ) yet he may have a confessors, he hath been ready to glorifie God, in the shedding of his blood. And if a woman cannot possess a virgins house (she hath embrac'd the holy state of marriage) yet she may have a matrons house, she hath brought forth, and brought up children in the fear of God. *In domo patris,* In my Fathers house, in heaven, there are many mansions, but here upon earth, *The Son of man hath not where to lay his head*, saies he himself. *Nonne terram dedit filiis hominum?* How then hath God given this earth to the Sons of men? He hath given them earth for their materials, to be made of earth; and he hath given them earth for their grave and

6

sepulture, to return and resolve to earth; but not for their possession. *Here we have no continuing City*; nay no Cottage that continues; nay, no persons, no bodies that continue. Whatsoever moved *St. Hierome* to call the journies of the Israelites in the wilderness, Mansions, the word, (the word is *nasang*) signifies but a journie, but a peregrination: even the Israel of God hath no mansions, but journies, pilgrimages in this life. By that measure did *Jacob* measure his life to *Pharaoh*, *The daies of the years of my pilgrimage*. And though the Apostle would not say, *morimur*, that whilst we are in the body, we are dead, yet he saies, *peregrinamur*, whilst we are in the body, we are but in a pilgrimage, and we are absent from the Lord. He might have said dead; for this whole world is but an universal Church-yard, but our common grave; and the life and motion, that the greatest persons have in it, is but as the shaking of buried bodies in their graves by an earthquake. That which we call life, is but *Hebdomada mortium*, a week of deaths, seaven daies, seaven periods of our life spent in dying; a dying seaven times over, and ther's an end. Our birth dies in Infancy, and our infancy dies in youth, and youth, and the rest die in age; and age also dies, and determines all. Nor do all these, youth out of infancy, or age out of youth, arise, so as a Phenix out of the ashes of another Phenix formerly dead, but as a wasp, or a serpent out of carrion, or as a snake out of dung; our youth is worse then our infancy, and our age worse then our youth; our youth is hungry and thirsty after those sins which our infancy knew not, and our age is sorry and angry that it cannot pursue those sins which our youth did. And besides, all the way so many deaths, that is, so many deadly calamities

Heb. 13. 14.

Exo. 17. 1.

Gen. 47. 9.

2 Cor. 5. 6.

7

accompany every condition, and every period of this life, as that death it self would be an ease to them that suffer them. Upon this sense does *Job* wish, that God had not given him an issue from the first death, from the womb; *Wherefore hast thou brought me forth out of the womb? O that I had given up the Ghost, and no eye had seen me; I should have been, as though I had not been.*

[Job] 10. 18.

And not only the impatient Israelites in their murmuring, (*would to God we had died by the hand of the Lord, in the land of Egypt*) but *Eliah* himself, when he fled from *Jezabel*, and went for his life, as that Text saies, under the juniper tree requested that he might die, and said, *It is enough, now O Lord take away my life.* So *Jonah* justifies his impatience, nay his anger towards God himself; *Now O Lord take I beseech thee my life from me, for it is better for me to die, then to live.* And when God ask'd him, *dost thou well to be angry for this*, and after, (about the Gourd) *dost thou well to be angry for that*, he replies, *I do well to be angry even unto death.* How much worse a death, then death is this life, which so good men would so often change for death? But if my case be St. *Pauls* case, *Quotidie morior*, that I die dayly, that something heavier then death fall upon me every day; If my case be *Davids* case, *Tota die mortificamur*, all the day long we are killed, that not only every day, but every hour of the day, something heavier then death fals upon me: though that be true of me, *conceptus in peccatis*, I was shapen in iniquity, and in sin did my mother conceive me, (There I died one death) though that be true of me, *natus filius iræ*, I was born, not only the child of sin, but the child of the wrath of God for sin, which is a heavier death, yet *Domini Domini sunt exitus*

Exo. 16. 3.

I Reg. 19. 4.

[Jon.] 4. 3.

I. Cor. 15. 31.

Psa. 44. 22.

51. 5.

[Eph. 2. 3.]

mortis, with God the Lord are the issues of death; and after a *Job*, and a *Joseph*, and a *Jeremy*, and a *Daniel*, I cannot doubt of a deliverance; and if no other deliverance conduce more to his glory, and my good, yet, *He hath the keyes of* Apoc. 1. 18. *death*, and he can let me out at that dore, that is, deliver me from the manifold deaths of this world, the *omni die*, and the *tota die*, the every daies death, and every hours death, by that one death, the final disolution of body and soul, the end of all.

But then, is that the end of all? is that dissolution of body and soul, the last death that the body shall suffer? (for of spiritual death we speak not now;) it is not. Though this be *exitus a morte*, it is *introitus in mortem*, though it be an issue *Exitus a morte Incinerationis.* from the manifold deaths of this world, yet it is an entrance into the death of corruption, and putrifaction, and vermiculation, and incineration, and dispersion, in, and from the grave, in which every dead man dies over again. It was a prerogative peculiar to Christ, not to die this death, not to see corruption. What gave him this privilege? not *Josephs* great proportions of gums and spices, that might have preserved his body from corruption and incineration, longer then he needed it, longer then three daies; but yet would not have done it for ever. What preserv'd him then? did his exemption, and freedome from original sin, preserve him from this corruption and incineration? 'Tis true, that original sin hath induc'd this corruption and incineration upon us. If we had not sinn'd in *Adam*, mortality had not put on immortality, 1 Cor. 15. 33. (as the Apostle speaks) nor corruption had not put on incorruption, but we had had our transmigration from this to the other world, without any mortality, any corruption at all.

But yet since Christ took sin upon him, so far as made him mortal, he had it so far too, as might have made him see this corruption and incineration, though he had no original sin in himself. What preserv'd him then? did the hypostatical union of both natures, God and man, preserve his flesh from this corruption, this incineration? 'tis true that this was a most powerful embalming: To be embalm'd with the divine nature it self, to be embalm'd with eternity, was able to preserve him from corruption and incineration for ever: And he was embalm'd so, embalm'd with the divine nature, even in his body, as well as in his soul; for the Godhead, the divine nature, did not depart, but remained still united to his dead body in the grave. But yet for all this powerful imbalming, this hypostatical union of both natures, we see, Christ did die; and for all this union which made him God and man, he became no man, (for, the union of body and soul makes the man, and he, whose soul and body are separated by death, (as long as that state lasts) is properly no man.) And therefore as in him, the dissolution of body and soul was no dissolution of the hypostatical union, so is there nothing that constrains us to say, that though the flesh of Christ had seen corruption and incineration in the grave, this had been any dissolution of the hypostatical union; for the divine nature, the Godhead might have remain'd with all the elements and principles of Christs body, as well as it did with the two constitutive parts of his person, his body and his soul. This incorruption then was not in *Josephs* gums and spices; nor was it in Christs innocency and exemption from original sin; nor was it, (that is, it is not necessary to say it was) in the Hypostatical union. But this incorruptibleness of his flesh, is most

conveniently plac'd in that, *non dabis, Thou wilt not suffer thy* Psa. 16. 10.
holy one to see corruption. We look no farther for causes or
reasons in the mysteries of our religion, but to the will and
pleasure of God. Christ himself limited his inquisition in
that; *Ita est*, even so, father, for so it seemed good in thy Mat. 11. 26.
sight. Christs body did not see corruption, therefore, because
God had decreed that it should not. The humble soul, (and
only the humble soul is the religious soul) rests himself upon
Gods purposes, and his decrees; but then, it is upon those
purposes, and decrees of God, which he hath declared and
manifested; not such as are conceiv'd and imagin'd in our
selves, though upon some probability, some verisimilitude.
So, in our present case, *Peter* proceeded in his sermon at Act. 2. 31.
Jerusalem, and so *Paul* in his at *Antioch*; they preached 13. 35.
Christ to be risen without having seen corruption, not only
because God had decreed it, but because he had manifested
that decree in his Prophet. Therefore does St. *Paul* cite by
special number the second *Psalme* for that decree, and therefore both St. *Peter* and St. *Paul* cite for that place in the
16. *Psal.* for, when God declares his decree and purpose in *ver.* 10.
the express word of his Prophet, or when he declares it in
the real execution of the decree, then he makes it ours, then
he manifests it to us. And therefore as the mysteries of our
religion are not the objects of our reason, but by faith we
rest on Gods decree and purpose, (it is so, O God, because it is
thy will it should be so) so Gods decrees are ever to be considered in the manifestation thereof. All manifestation is
either in the word of God, or in the execution of the decree;
and when these two concur and meet, it is the strongest de-
monstration that can be: when therefore I find those marks

of Adoption, and spiritual filiation, which are delivered in the word of God, to be upon me; when I find that real execution of his good purpose upon me, as that actually I do live under the obedience, and under the conditions which are evidences of adoption and spiritual filiation, then, and so long as I see these marks, and live so, I may safely comfort my self in a holy certitude, & a modest infallibility of my adoption. Christ determins h'mself in that, the purpose of God; because the purpose of God was manifest to him: St. *Peter* and St. *Paul*, determine themselves in those two waies of knowing the purpose of God, the word of God before, the execution of the Decree in the fulness of time. It was prophecied before, said they, & it is perform'd now; Christ is risen without seeing corruption.

Now this which is so singularly peculiar to him, that his flesh should not see corruption, at his second coming, his coming to Judgment, shall be extended to all that are then alive, their flesh shall not see corruption; because (as the 1 Cor. 15. 51. Apostle saies, and saies as a secret, as a mystery, *behold I shew you a mystery*) *we shall not all sleep*, (that is, not continue in the state of the dead in the grave) *but we shall all be changed*. In an instant we shall have a dissolution, and in the same instant a redintegration, a recompacting of body and soul; and that shall be truly a death, and truly a resurrection, but no sleeping, no corruption. But for us, who dy now, and sleep in the state of the dead, we must all pass this posthume death, this death after death, nay this death after burial, this dissolution after dissolution, this death of corruption and putrefaction, of vermiculation and incineration of dissolution and dispersion, in, and from the grave. When those

12

bodies which have been the children of royal Parents, and the Parents of royal Children, must say with *Job, to corrup-* Job. 17. 14. *tion thou art my Father, & to the worm thou art my Mother & my Sister.* Miserable riddle, when the same worm must be my mother, & my sister, & my self. Miserable incest, when I must be married to mine own mother and sister, and be 24. 20. both Father and Mother, to mine owne mother and sister, beget and bear that worm, which is all that miserable penury, when my mouth shall be filled with dust, and the worm shall feed, and feed sweetly upon me. When the ambitious man shall have no satisfaction if the poorest alive tread upon him, nor the poorest receive any contentment, in being made equal to Princes, for they shall be equal but in dust. One dyeth at his full strength, being wholly at ease, and in 21. 23. quiet, and another dies in the bitterness of his soul, and never eats with pleasure; but they ly down alike in the dust, and the worm covers them. The worm covers them in *Job,* and in *Esai,* it covers them, & is spread under them, the [Esa.] 14. 11. worm is spread under thee, and the worm covers thee. There is the mats and the carpet that lie under; and there is the state and the canopy that hangs over the greatest of the Sons of men. Even those bodies that were the Temples of the holy Ghost, come to this dilapidation, to ruine, to rubbish, to dust: Even the Israel of the Lord, and *Jacob* himself had no other specification, no other denomination but that, *vermis* Esa. 41. 14. *Jacob,* thou worm of *Jacob.* Truly, the consideration of this posthume death, this death after burial, that after God, with whom are the issues of death, hath delivered me from the death of the womb, by bringing me into the world, and from the manifold deaths of the world, by laying me in the grave.

13

I must die again, in an incineration of this flesh, and in a dispersion of that dust: That that monarch who spread over many nations alive, must in his dust lie in a corner of that sheet of lead, and there but so long as the lead will last: and that private and retired man, that thought himself his own for ever, and never came forth, must in his dust of the grave be published, and, (such are the revolutions of graves) be mingled in his dust, with the dust of every high way, and of every dunghil, and swallowed in every puddle and pond; this is the most inglorious and contemptible villification, the most deadly and peremptory nullification of man, that we can consider. God seems to have carried the declaration of his power to a great heighth, when he sets the Prophet [Esa.] 37. 1. *Ezechiel*, in the valley of dry bones, and saies, *Son of man can these dry bones live?* as though it had been impossible; and yet they did; the Lord laid sinews upon them, and flesh, and breathed into them, and they did live. But in that case there were bones to be seen; something visible, of which it might be said, can this thing live? but in this death of incineration and dispersion of dust, we see nothing that we can call that mans. If we say can this dust live? perchance it cannot. It may be the meer dust of the earth which never did live, nor never shall; it may be the dust of that mans worms which did live, but shall no more; it may be the dust of another man that concerns not him of whom it is asked. This death of incineration and dispersion is to natural reason the most irrecoverable death of all; and yet *Domini Domini sunt exitus mortis*, unto God the Lord belong the issues of death, and by recompacting this dust into the same body, and re-inanimating the same body with the same soul, he shall in a blessed and glorious Resurrection, give me such an issue from this Death, as shall never passe into any other death, but establish me in a Life, that shall last as long as the Lord of Life himself. And so have you that that belongs to the first acceptation of these words (*unto God the Lord belong the issues of Death*). That though from the womb to the grave, and in the grave it self, we passe from Death to Death, yet, as *Daniel* speaks, The Lord our God is able to deliver us, and he will deliver us. And so we passe to our second accomodation of these words (*Unto God the Lord belong the issues of Death*) That it belongs to God, and not to Man, to passe a Judgement upon us at our Death, or to conclude a dereliction on God's part, upon the manner thereof.

THOSE indications which Physitians receive, and those presagitions which they give for death or recovery in the Patient, they receive, and they give out of the grounds and rules of their Art: But we have no such rule or art to ground a presagition of spiritual death, and damnation upon any such indication as we see in any dying man: we see often enough to be sorry, but not to despayr; for the mercies of God work momentanely, in minuts; and many times insensibly to by-standers, or any other then the party departing, and we may be deceived both wayes: we use to comfort our selves in the death of a friend, if it be testifyed that he went away like a Lamb, that is, without any reluctation; But God knows, that may have been accompanied with a dangerous damp and stupefaction, and insensibility of his present state. Our blessed Saviour suffered colluctations with Death,

Part 2.
Liberatio in morte.

15

and a sadnesse even in his Soul to death, and an agony even to a bloody sweat in his body, and expostulations with God, and exclamations upon the Crosse. He was a devout man, who upon his death-bed, or death-turfe (for he was an Hermit) said *Septuaginta annos domino servivisti, & mori times?* Hast thou serv'd a good Master three score and ten yeeres, and now art thou loth to goe into his presence? yet *Hilarion* was loath. He was a devoute man (an *Hermite* too) that said that day he died, *Cogitate hodie cæpisse servire Domino, & hodie finiturum.* Consider this to be the first days service that ever thou didst thy Master to gloryfie him in a christianly and constant death; and, if thy first day be thy last too, how soone dost thou come to receive thy wages; yet *Barlaam* could have beene content to have stayed longer for it; Make no ill conclusion upon any man's lothnesse to die. And then, upon violent deaths inflicted, as upon malefactors, Christ himself hath forbidden us by his own death to make any ill conclusions; for, his own death had those impressions in it; he was reputed, he was executed as a Malefactor, and no doubt many of them who concurred to his death, did beleeve him to be so. Of sodain deaths, there are scarce examples; to be found in the Scriptures, upon good men; for, death in battail cannot be called sodain death: But God governs not by examples, but by rules; and therefore make no ill conclusions upon sodain-Death; nor upon distempers neyther, though perchance accompanied with some words of diffidence and distrust in the mercies of God. The Tree lies as it falls; 'Tis true; but yet it is not the last stroke that fells the Tree; nor the last word, nor last gaspe that qualifies the Soule. Still pray we for a peaceable life, against violent

Hilarion.

Barlaam.

[Eccles. 11. 3.]

16

deaths, and for time of Repentance against sodaine Deaths, and for sober and modest assurance against distemper'd and diffident Deaths, but never make ill conclusions upon persons overtaken with such Deaths. *Domini, Domini sunt exitus Mortis*, To God the Lord belong the issues of Death, and he received *Samson*, who went out of this world in such a manner (consider it actively, consider it passively; in his own death, and in those whom he slew with himself) as was subject to interpretation hard enough; yet the holy-Ghost hath mov'd Saint *Paul* to celebrate *Samson*, in his great Cata- Heb. 11. [32.] logue, and so doth all the Church. Our Criticall day is not the very day of our death, but the whole course of our life: I thank him, that prayes for me when my bell tolls; but I thank him much more, that Catechises me, or preaches to me, or instructs me how to live, *fac hoc & vives*, There's my [Luk. 10. 28.] security; The mouth of the Lord hath spoken it, *Doe this and thou shalt live*. But though I doe it yet I shall die too, dy a bodily, a naturall death; but God never mentions, never seems to consider that death, the bodily, the naturall death. God doth not say Live well, and thou shalt die well, that is, an easy, a quiet death; but live well here, and thou shalt live well for ever. As the first part of a Sentence peeces well with the last, and never respects, never hearkens after the parenthesis that comes between, so doth a good life here, flow into an eternall life, without any consideration what manner of death we die. But whether the gate of my prison be opened with an oyl'd key (by a gentle and preparing sicknesse) or the gate be hew'd down, by a violent death, or the gate be burnt down by a rageing and frantick feaver; a gate into Heaven I shall have; for, from the Lord is the cause of my

17

life, and with God the Lord are the issues of death; And farther we carry not this second acceptation of the words, as this issue of death is *liberatio in morte*, God's care that the Soule be safe, what agonie soever the body suffers in the houre of death; but passe to our third and last Part; as this issue of death is *liberatio per mortem*, a deliverance by the death of another, by the death of Christ.

Part 3.
Liberatio per mortem.

UFFERENTIAM Job audiistis & vidistis finem Domini, saies S. *James* 5. 11. You have heard of the patience of *Job*, saies he; All this while you have done that; for in every man, calamitous, miserable man a *Job* speaks; *Now see the end of the Lord*, saith that Apostle, which is not that end that the Lord proposed to himself (Salvation to us) nor the end which he proposes to us (conformity to him) but, *See the end of the Lord* saies he, the end that the Lord himself came to, Death, and a painfull, and a shamefull death. But why did he die? and why die so? *Quia Domini Domini sunt exitus Mortis* (as Saint *Augustine* interpreting this Text, answers that question) because to this God our Lord belong'd the issues of Death; *Quid apertius diceretur?* sayes he there; what can be more obvious, more manifest, then this sense of these words? In the former part of this verse it is said, *He that is our God is the God of Salvation; Deus salvos faciendi*, so he reads it, The God that must save us; Who can that be, saith he, but Jesus? For therefore that name was given him, because he was to save us: And to this Jesus, saith he, this Saviour, belongs the issues of Death, *Nec oportuit eum de hac vita alios exitus habere, quam mortis,*

De Civit. Dei
lib. 17. c. 18.

Mat. 1. 21.

18

Being come into this life in our mortall nature, he could not goe out of it any other way then by Death. *Ideo dictum* (saith he) therefore is it said, *To God the Lord belong the issues of Death; Ut ostenderetur moriendo nos salvos facturum*, to shew that his way to save us, was to die. And from this Text doth Saint *Isiodore* prove, that Christ was truly man (which, as many Sects of Hereticks denied, as that he was truly God) because to him, though he were *Dominus Dominus* (as the Text doubles it) God the Lord, yet to him, to God the Lord belong'd the issues of Death. *Oportuit eum pati*, more cannot be said, then Christ himself saith of himself, *These things Christ ought to suffer*; He had no other way but by Death. So Luk. 24. 26. then, this part of our Sermon must needes be a Passion Sermon, since all his life was a continuall Passion, all our Lent may well be a continual good-Friday; Christ's painfull Life took off none of the pains of his Death; he felt not the lesse then, for having felt so much before; nor will any thing that shall be said before, lessen, but rather enlarge your devotion to that which shall be said of his Passion, at the time of the due solemnization thereof. Christ bled not a drop the lesse at the last, for having bled at his Circumcision before, nor will you shed a teare the lesse then, if you shed some now. And therefore be now content to consider with me, how to this *God the Lord belong'd the issues of Death*.

That *God* this *Lord*, The Lord of Life could die, is a strange contemplation; That the red-Sea could be dry; That *Potuisse Mori.* the Sun could stand still; That an Oven could be seven times Exod. 14. 21.
Jos. 10. 12. heat and not burn; That Lyons could be hungry and not [Dan. 3. 19.
6. 22.] bite, is strange, miraculously strange; But super-miraculous, That God could die: But that God would die, is an exaltation of that; But, even of that also, it is a super-exaltation, that God should die, must die; and *non exitus* (saith Saint *Augustin*) God the Lord had no issue but by death, and *oportuit pati* (saith Christ himself) all this Christ ought to suffer, was bound to suffer. *Deus ultionum Deus*, saith *David*, God is the God of Revenges; He would not passe over the sin of man unrevenged, unpunished. But then, *Deus ultionum libere egit* (sayes that place). The God of Revenges works freely; he punishes, he spares whom he will; and would he not spare himself? He would not. *Dilectio fortis Mortus*, Love is strong as Death; stronger; it drew in Death, that naturally was not welcome. *Si possibile* (saith Christ) *If it be possible let this cup passe*, when his Love, expressed in a former Decree with his Father, had made it impossible. Many waters quench not Love; Christ tryed many; He was baptized out of his Love, and his love determin'd not there; He wept over *Jerusalem* out of his love, and his love determined not there; He mingled blood with water in his Agony and that determined not his love; He wept pure blood, all his blood, at all his eyes, at all his pores; in his flagellation, and thornes; (to the Lord our God belonged the issues of blood) and these expressed, but these did not quench his love.

He would not spare, nay, he would not spare himself; There was nothing more free, more voluntary, more spontaneous then the death of Christ; 'Tis true, *libere egit*, he died voluntarily; But yet, when we consider the contract that had passed between his Father and him, there was an *Oportuit*, a kinde of necessity upon him. All this Christ ought to suffer; And when shall we date this obligation, this *Oportuit*,

Psa. 94. 1.
Voluisse Mori.

Cant. 8. 6.

[Mat. 26. 39.]

Ver. 7.

Oportuisse Mori.

20

this necessity, when shall we say it begun? Certainly this Decree by which Christ was to suffer all this, was an eternall Decree; and was there any thing before that that was eternall? Infinite love, eternall love; be pleased to follow this home, and to consider it seriously, that what liberty soever we can conceive in Christ, to dy, or not to dy, this necessity of dying, this Decree is as eternall as that Liberty, and yet how small a matter made he of this Necessity, and this dying? His Father calls it but a Bruise, and but a bruising of his heele (*The Serpent shall bruise his heele*) and yet that was, Gen. 3. 15. that the Serpent should practise and compasse his death. Himself calls it but a Baptism, as though he were to be the better for it; *I have a Baptism to be Baptized with*; and he was Luk. 12. 50. in paine till it was accomplished; and yet this Baptism was his death. The holy-Ghost calls it Joy (*For the joy which was set* Heb. 12. 2. *before him, he endured the Crosse*) which was not a joy of his reward after his passion, but a joy that filled him even in the middest of those torments, and arose from them. When Christ cals his passion *Calicem*, a cup, and no worse, (*Can ye* Mat. 20. 22. *drink of my cup*;) He speaks not odiously, not with detestation of it; indeed it was a cup; *salus mundo*, A health to all the world; and *quid retribuem*, saies *David*, *What shall I render unto the Lord?* Answer you with *David*, *Accipiam Calicem*, Psa. 116. 12. I will take the cup of salvation. Take that, that cup of salvation his passion, if not into your present imitation, yet into your present contemplation, and behold how that Lord who was God yet could die, would die, must die for your salvation.

That *Moses* and *Elias* talked with Christ in the trans- Mat. 17. 3. figuration both St. *Matthew*, and St. *Mark* tel us; but what Mar. 9. 4.

they talked of, only St. *Luke*; *Dicebant excessum ejus*, saies he; they talked of his decease, of his death, which was to be accomplished at *Jerusalem*. The word is of his *Exodus*, the very word of our Text, *Exitus*, his issue by death. *Moses*, who in his *Exodus* had prefigured this issue of our Lord, and in passing Israel out of *Egypt* through the red sea, had foretold in that actual prophecy Christs passing of mankind through the sea of his blood, and *Elias*, whose *Exodus*, and issue out of this world, was a figure of Christs ascension, had no doubt a great satisfaction, in talking with our blessed Lord, *De excessu ejus*, of the full consummation of all this in his death, which was to be accomplished at *Jerusalem*. Our meditation of his death should be more visceral, and affect us more, because it is of a thing already done. The ancient Romans had a certain tenderness, and detestation of the name of death; they would not name death, no not in their wils; there they would not say, *Si mori contingerit*, but *Si quid humanitas contingat*, not if or when I die, but when the course of nature is accomplished upon me. To us, that speak daily of the death of Christ, (He was crucified, dead and buried) can the memory or the mention of our own death be irksome or bitter? There are in these latter times amongst us, that name death freely enough, and the death of God, but in blasphemus oaths and execrations. Miserable men, who shall therefore be said never to have named Jesus, because they have named him too often; and therefore hear Jesus say, *Nescivi vos* I never knew you; because they made themselves too familiar with him. *Moses* and *Elias* talked with Christ of his death, only in a holy and joyful sense of the benefit which they and all the world were to receive by that. Discourses of

22

religion should not be out of curiosity, but to edification. And then they talked with Christ of his death, at that time when he was at the greatest heighth of glory, that ever he admitted in this world; that is, his transfiguration. And we are afraid to speak to the great men of this world of their death, but nourish in them a vain imagination of immortallity and immutability. But *bonum est nobis esse hic*, (as St. *Peter* said there) It is good to dwell here, in this consideration of his death, and therefore transfer we our Tabernacle, (our devotions) through some of those steps, which God the Lord made to his issue of death, that day.

Take in his whole day, from the hour that Christ eat the *Conformitas.* passover upon Thursday, to the hour in which he died the next day. Make this present day, that day in thy devotion, and consider what he did, and remember what you have done. Before he instituted and celebrated the sacrament, (which was after the eating of the passover) he proceeded to the act of humility, to wash his Disciples feet; even *Peters*, who for a while resisted him. In thy preparation to the holy and blessed sacrament, hast thou with a sincere humility sought a reconciliation with all the world, even with those who have been averse from it, and refused that reconciliation from thee? If so, (and not else) thou hast spent that first part, of this his last day, in a conformity with him. After the sacrament, he spent the time til night in prayer, in preaching, in Psalms. Hast thou considered that a worthy receiving of the sacrament consists in a continuation of holiness after, as wel as in a preparation before? If so, thou hast therein also conformed thy self to him: so Christ spent his time till night. At night he went into the garden to pray, and

23

Luk. 22. 44.

he prayed *prolixius*; He spent much time in prayer. How much? because it is literally expressed that he praied there three several times, and that returning to his Disciples after

Mat. 26. 40.

his first prayer, and finding them asleep, said, *could ye not watch with me one hour*; it is collected that he spent three houres in prayer. I dare scarce ask thee whither thou wentst, or how thou disposedst of thy self, when it grew dark and after last night. If that time were spent in a holy recommendation of thy self to God, and a submission of thy will to his, it was spent in a conformity to him. In that time, and in those prayers was his agony and bloody sweat. I will hope that thou didst pray; but not every ordinary and customary prayer, but prayer actually accompanied with shedding of tears, and dispositively, in a readiness to shed blood for his glory in necessary cases, puts thee into a conformity with him. About midnight he was taken and bound with a kiss. Art thou not too conformable to him in that? Is not that too literally, too exactly thy case? At midnight to have been taken, and bound with a kiss? From thence he was carried back to *Jerusalem*; first to *Annas*, then to *Caiphas*, and, (as late as it was) then he was examined, and buffeted, and delivered over to the custody of those officers, from whom he received all those irrisions, and violences, the covering of his face, the spitting upon his face, the blasphemies of words, and the smartness of blows which that Gospel mentions. In which compass fell that *Gallicinium*, that crowing of the Cock, which called up *Peter* to his repentance. How thou passedst all that time last night, thou knowest. If thou didst any thing then that needed *Peters* tears, and hast not shed them, let me be thy Cock, do it now; now thy Master, (in the unworthyest of his servants) looks back upon thee, Do it now. Betimes in the morning, as soon as it was day, the Jews held a Councel in the high Priests house, and agreed upon their evidence against him, & then carried him to *Pilate*, who was to be his Judg. Didst thou accuse thy self when thou wak'dst this morning, & wast thou content to admit even fals accusations, that is, rather to suspect actions to have been sin which were not, then to smother & justifie such as were truly sins? then thou spendst that hour in conformity to him. *Pilat* found no evidence against him; & therefore to ease himself, & to pass a complement upon *Herod*, Tetrarch of *Galilee*, who was at that time at *Jerusalem*, (because Christ being a *Galilean* was of *Herods* jurisdiction) *Pilat* sent him to *Herod*; & rather as a mad man, then a malefactor, *Herod* remanded him with scorns to *Pilat* to proceed against him; & this was about 8 of the Clock. Hast thou been content to come to this inquisition, this examination, this agitation, this cribration, this pursuit of thy conscience, to sift it, to follow it from the sins of thy youth to thy present sins, from the sins of thy bed to the sins of thy board, and from the substance to the circumstance of thy sins; that's time spent like thy Saviours. *Pilat* would have sav'd Christ by using the priviledg of the day in his behalf, because that day one prisoner was to be delivered; but they chose *Barrabas*. He would have sav'd him from death, by satisfying their fury, with inflicting other torments upon him, scourging, and crowning with thorns, & loading him with many scornful & ignominious contumelies; but this redeem'd him not; they press'd a crucifying. Hast thou gone about to redeem thy sin, by fasting, by alms, by disciplines, & mortifications, in the way of

25

satisfaction to the justice of God; that will not serve, that's not the right way. We press an utter crucifying of that sin that governs thee, and that conforms thee to Christ. Towards noon *Pilat* gave Judgment; and they made such hast to execution, as that by noon he was upon the Cross. There now hangs that sacred body upon the cross, re-baptiz'd in his own tears & sweat, and embalm'd in his own blood alive. There are those bowels of compassion, which are so conspicuous, so manifested, as that you may see them through his wounds. There those glorious eyes grew faint in their light, so as the Sun asham'd to survive them, departed with his light too. And there that Son of God, who was never from us, & yet had now come a new way unto us, in assuming our nature, delivers that soul which was never out of his Father's hands, into his Father's hands, by a new way, a voluntary emission thereof; for though to *this God our Lord belong'd these issues of death*, so that, considered in his own contract, he must necessarily dy, yet at no breach, or battery which they had made upon his sacred body issued his soul, but *emisit*, he gave up the Ghost: & as God breath'd a soul into the first *Adam*, so this second *Adam* breath'd his soul into God, into the hands of God. There we leave you, in that blessed dependancy, to hang upon him, that hangs upon the cross. There bath in his tears, there suck at his wounds, & lie down in peace in his grave, till he vouchsafe you a Resurrection, & an ascension into that Kingdome which he hath purchas'd for you, with the inestimable price of his incorruptible blood.

AMEN.

26

EDITOR'S
POSTSCRIPT

JOHN DONNE, poet and preacher, was born in London in 1572. During his secular life he had no conscious vocation for the Church and was not ordained deacon and priest until January 1615 – and then only at the instance, almost at the command, of King James. The King had been greatly impressed by the learning and sound doctrinal principles shewn in Donne's first book, *Pseudo-Martyr*, published in 1610; in this now almost unreadable treatise[1] Donne was at pains to prove that Roman Catholics should take the oath of allegiance to the King, their refusal to do so only bringing on themselves the punishment due for those who would not recognize their lawful sovereign. As recusants they suffered nothing but self-inflicted pseudo-martyrdom. Donne had proved by this work his unquestionable suitability for ecclesiastical preferment, and he finally submitted to the King's persuasions five years after the appearance of his book.

Donne's later career proved how right King James had been in his opinion, although this was founded primarily on political expediency. His life as a Churchman was devoted wholly to propagation of the Christian religion without self-seeking or administrative chicanery, turning the whole of his formidable intellect onto the composition of sermons and devotional poetry, but more particularly to the sermons, by which he became known as by far the greatest preacher of his century. His fame has, indeed, remained undimmed for almost 350 years, until now, in the quatercentenary year of his birth, it would be difficult to name any preacher who has ever excelled his distinction in the pulpit. Nevertheless Donne approached his duties as a preacher

---

[1] But I am assured by the distinguished historian, Dr. A. L. Rowse, that he has read it through with great interest and satisfaction.

with diffidence and reluctance. Izaak Walton, his first biographer, described this gradual development with convincing eloquence:

> Though his long familiarity with Scholars, and persons of greatest quality, was such as might have given some men boldness enough to have preached to any eminent Auditory, yet his modesty in this imployment was such, that he could not be perswaded to it, but went usually accompanied with some one friend, to preach privately in some village, not far from *London*: his first Sermon being preached at *Paddington*. This he did, till His Majesty sent and appointed him a day to preach to him at *White-hall*, and, though much were expected from him, both by His Majesty and others, yet he was so happy (which few are) as to satisfie and exceed their expectations: preaching the Word so, as shewed his own heart was possest with those very thoughts and joyes that he labored to distill into others: A Preacher in earnest, weeping sometimes for his Auditory, sometimes with them: always preaching to himself, like an Angel from a cloud, but in none; carrying some, as St. *Paul* was, to Heaven in holy raptures, and inticing others by a sacred Art and Courtship to amend their lives; here picturing a vice so as to make it ugly to those that practised it; and a vertue so, as to make it be beloved even by those that lov'd it not; and, all this with a most particular grace and an unexpressible addition of comeliness.[1]

The first of Donne's sermons to be published was preached at St. Paul's Cross on 15 September 1622, more than seven years after his ordination. Even then it did not give universal satisfaction, as was recorded by a contemporary commentator, John Chamberlain, who advised a correspondent that:

> On the 15th of this present the Dean of Paules preached at the Crosse to certifie the Kings goode intention in the late orders concerning preachers and preaching, and of his constancie in the true reformed religion, which the people (as shold seeme) began to suspect; his text was the 20th verse of the 5th chapter of the booke of Judges, somewhat a straunge text for such a business, and how he made yt

[1] All quotations are taken from Walton's *Lives*, London, 1670.

hold together I know not, but he gave no great satisfaction, or as some say spake as yf himself were not so well satisfied.[1]

But again it was the King's wish to defend his own position through Donne's mouth that gave it the flavour of unreality expressed by Chamberlain. Donne's progression as a preacher can, however, be traced through the general body of his sermons, of which 160 are extant; six were printed during his lifetime between 1622 and 1627, and seven more appeared soon after his death. Finally three folio volumes, edited by his son, John Donne D.C.L., containing the last seven sermons together with 147 previously unpublished, appeared in the years 1640, 1649 and 1660.

Evidence in plenty has therefore survived in print to enable us to perceive how difficult even Donne found it to adjust his powerful mind to the needs of his dissimilar audiences. His latest biographer, R. C. Bald, noted that, in 1615, after Donne had preached for the first time before a congregation at the Inns of Court one of his hearers wrote to a friend:

> this day Mr donn preached att our temple; he had to much learninge for ignoramus.[2]

Bald also found that an earlier sermon preached on 30 April of the same year had an uneven style, parts of it approaching the 'bareness' of Bishop Lancelot Andrewes, while other parts shewed a tendency to develop more elaborate rhetoric. His chief object seemed to be to offer an interpretation of scripture with little advice or exhortation to his audience.

There can be no doubt that, with experience, Donne became able to modify his style and matter to suit gatherings of people drawn variously from his parishioners at St. Dunstan's in the Strand, from the people of London who came to hear the Dean of St. Paul's in his Cathedral, from country people in villages around London, or from the royal Court, including the King himself,

When Donne's collected *Poems* were published in 1633, two years after his death, a number of his friends and admirers contributed

---

[1] *Letters of John Chamberlain*, ed. McClure, Philadelphia, 1939, ii, p. 518.
[2] *Life of Donne*, Oxford, 1970, p. 312.

29

'Elegies upon the Author' and from these it is possible to gather a variety of opinions on his powers as a preacher. Most of them praised him as a poet, his secular verses being very much in their minds. Sir Edward Hyde (afterwards Lord Clarendon) neatly concluded his contribution by combining his poetry with his theology in the lines:

> Hee then must write, that would define thy parts:
> *Here lyes the best Divinitie, All the Arts.*

Several others in this solemn chorus of praise referred more specifically to Donne's preaching. Henry Valentine a royalist clergyman, after bearing witness to the loss that poetry had suffered, continued:

> They [the Muses] shall have *Ballads*, but no *Poetry*.
> *Language* lyes speechlesse, and *Divinity*,
> Lost such a *Trump* as even to *Extasie*
> Could charme the Soule, and had an *Influence*
> To teach best *judgements*, and please dullest *Sense*.
> The *Court*, the *Church*, the *Universitie*,
> Lost *Chaplaine*, *Deane*, and *Doctor*, All these, Three.

Sir Lucius Carie, Viscount Falkland, a man, according to the great Lord Clarendon, of much distinction and charm, painted an impression of the preacher in the lines:

> Nor was there expectation to gain grace
> From forth his Sermons only, but his face;
> So Primitive a looke, such gravitie
> With humblenesse, and both with Pietie;
> So milde was Moses countenance, when he prai'd,
> For them whose Satanisme his power gainsaid;
> And such his gravitie, when all Gods band
> Receiv'd his word (through him) at second hand,
> Which joyn'd, did flames of more devotion move
> Then ever Argive Hellens could of love.

Jasper Mayne, an Oxford scholar, but an indifferent poet, after ridiculing the ordinary preacher, continued in praise of Donne:

> Then should I praise thee, through the Tongues, and Arts,
> And have that deepe Divinity, to know,

What mysteries did from thy preaching flow,
Who with thy words could charme thy audience,
That at thy sermons, eare was all our sense;
Yet I have seene thee in the pulpit stand,
Where wee might take notes, from thy looke, and hande;
And from thy speaking action beare away
More sermon, then some teachers use to say.
Such was thy carriage, and thy gesture such,
As could divide the heart, and conscience touch.
Thy motion did confute, and wee might see
An error vanquish'd by delivery.
Not like our Sonnes of Zeale, who to reforme
Their hearers, fiercely at the Pulpit storme,
And beate the cushion into worse estate,
Then if they did conclude it reprobate,
Who can outpray the glasse, then lay about
Till all Predestination be runne out,
And from the point such tedious uses draw,
Their repetitions would make Gospell, Law.
No, In such temper would thy Sermons flow,
So well did Doctrine, and thy language show,
And had that holy feare, as, hearing thee,
The Court would mend, and a good Christian bee.

Next, 'Mr. R. B.', most probably Richard Busby[1], then a tutor at Christ Church, Oxford, afterwards the famous headmaster of Westminster School, recalled vividly his impression of the preacher:

Mee thinkes I see him in the pulpit standing,
Not eares, or eyes, but all mens hearts commanding,
Where wee that heard him, to our selves did faine
Golden Chrysostome was alive againe;
And never were we wearied, till we saw
His houre (and but an houre) to end did draw.

[1] Identified by Giles Oldisworth; see note below on p. 44.

He then compared Donne to 'the doctrine-men', or puritans, who

> ...humm'd against him; And with face most sowre
> Call'd him a strong lin'd man, a Macaroon,

and so on, to their disadvantage. Lastly there is the remarkable passage in the long Latin 'Elegy' added to the second edition of the *Poems* in 1635 by Daniel Darnelly, a country parson from Somerset with another cure nearer London in Hertfordshire. These lines have been rendered into English as follows by William R. LeFanu, lately Librarian to the Royal College of Surgeons of England:

> I have seen,
> I have heard and marvelled how in Paul's Church
> Men lifted up their hearts and eyes, whensoever the Preacher rose
> And held them by his wondrous gravity; like a Patriarch
> He poured forth words sweeter far than honey.
> At first he astounds his hearers, expounding mysteries
> Unheard before and not yet comprehended; they reflect
> In wonder and stand silent, eagerly listening.
> Soon, changing his manner and his style of speech,
> He treats of sorrows: fate and the mournful time
> Of death, and the return of our bodies to their primal ashes.
> Then mightest thou see all men groaning and grieving;
> One perchance does not refrain from weeping and
> Tears flow freely from his eyes. The Heavenly Father
> Desired his people thus to attend and surrender,
> To rouse their affections and put them at the bidding
> Of the famous voice, while it recites the oracles
> Of God's will from the high pulpit in power and mastery.

Donne's total quality was summed up by Thomas Carie, or Carew, poet and 'sewer-in-ordinary' to King Charles the First, in the epitaph:

> *Here lies a King, that rul'd as hee thought fit*
> *The Universall Monarchy of wit;*
> *Here lie two Flamens, and both those, the best,*
> *Apollo's first, at last, the true Gods Priest.*

These several witnesses provide an image of Donne, the strong-voiced Monarch of Wit, in the pulpit, reducing men to tears and sinners to repentance, underlining the truth of Izaak Walton's beautifully phrased description in his *Life of Donne*.

In the early seventeenth century the composition and delivery of sermons was an important intellectual exercise both for preacher and for audience, and the chief exponents of the art were expected to obey certain rules. A sermon must be composed with serious thought and frequent reference to the Fathers of the Church. It might be set down on paper as notes, or sometimes written out as a full draft ready for printing after delivery, but it must be committed to memory and never read by any preacher of repute, even though it lasted for at least an hour or even more. In this connexion Walton wrote of Donne that,

> The latter part of his life may be said to be a continued study; for as he usually preached once a week, if not oftner, so after his Sermon he never gave his eyes rest, till he had chosen out a new Text, and that night cast his Sermon into a form, and his Text into divisions; and the next day betook himself to consult the Fathers, and so commit his meditations to his memory, which was excellent.

John Sparrow, Warden of All Souls College in Oxford,[1] has gathered ample evidence confirming the truth of this account of the principles governing the delivery of sermons by Donne and his contemporaries. He found evidence that sometimes Donne would write out the sermon before preaching it and make a fresh copy afterwards, this being what he called an 'ex-scribed copy'. In a letter written in 1627 to a friend, Robert Ker, Donne said that he knew that any good preacher 'had weighed every syllable for half a year before', and was speaking entirely from memory. Walton in his *Life of Dr. Sanderson, late Bishop of Lincoln*, 1678, wrote that Sanderson's sermons, though much esteemed, were less valued because he read them; though his memory was good, his 'invincible fear and bashfulness' was such that he could not trust it. Again, Joseph Hall, Bishop of Norwich, a celebrated preacher and a close friend of Donne, was in the habit of preaching three times in

[1] *Essays and Studies by Members of the English Association*, vol. XVI, Oxford, 1931, pp. 144–78.

a week, 'yet', he said, 'never durst I climbe into the Pulpit to preach any sermon, whereof I had not in my poor and plain fashion, penned every word in the same order wherein I hoped to deliver it, although in the expression I listed not to be a slave to syllables'.

Donne had been ordained early in 1615 and preached his first sermon soon afterwards. During the following sixteen years until his death on 31 March 1631 he preached many more sermons than the 160 that have survived in print. Walton said that he preached 'once a week, if not oftner'. This statement taken literally would mean that he delivered more than eight hundred sermons, but this is unlikely to be true. Walton's estimate that at his death he 'left six score of his sermons all written with his own hand' is more easy to believe. Against this may be set the letter written to Walton by Dr. Henry King, Donne's friend and executor, that he had been given the sermons afterwards published by the younger Donne, the father professing that 'it was by my restless importunity that he had prepared them for the press; together with which (as his best Legacy) he gave me all his sermon-Notes and his other Papers, containing an Extract of near Fifteen hundred Authours'. All these papers were afterwards borrowed by the younger Donne, using Walton as intermediary, and were never returned. Yet the son cannot be seriously blamed for this, since he proceeded with their systematic publication in the three folios of 1640, 1649 and 1660. Had they remained with Henry King, while he was Bishop of Chichester, it is unlikely that he could have done this, and, as pointed out by Professor Bald, the papers would probably have been destroyed when Cromwell's troops overran the Bishop's palace at Chichester in 1643. Moreover, the younger Donne had his father's authority for claiming that the sermons had been written out for his use should he take holy orders, as, indeed, he did in 1638.[1]

THE circumstances in which Donne preached his sermons and how they came to be preserved have been briefly examined in the foregoing pages. It remains to relate the story of his last appearance in the pulpit and of how he prepared to solemnize his death-bed scene, followed by details of the publication of his final and

[1] R. C. Bald, *Life of Donne*, 1970, p. 532.

most famous sermon, entitled *Deaths Duell*, and an examination of its substance.

In 1623 Donne experienced his first serious illness and for a time had believed that he would die. His life was certainly in danger, yet he remained a close observer of his own symptoms and mental reactions, recording them in a volume of Meditations and Prayers published in 1624 as *Devotions upon Emergent Occasions*. In the 16th Meditation is a sentence suggested to his feverish mind by the tolling of a bell in an adjoining church, by which, he wrote,

I am daily remembered of my buriall in the funerals of others.

This led to many reflections on funerals and tolling bells, and in the 17th Meditation under the heading:

Now, this Bell tolling softly for another, sayes to mee Thou must die,

Donne wrote:

Perchance hee for whom this *bell* tolls, may bee so ill, as that he knowes not it tolls for him,

and added on a later page:

The *Bell*, doth toll for him that *thinkes* it doth; and though it *intermit* againe, yet from that minute, that that occasion wrought upon him, he is united to *God*.

The sound of the tolling bell remained with him and, when writing his last sermon before his death, while he was again very ill, he seemed to hear it again when he said,

I thanke him that *prayes* for me when my bell tolls, but I thanke him much more that *Catechises* mee, or *preaches* to mee, or *instructs mee how to live*.

During the year 1630 Donne preached but seldom, though he was still active in his duties as Dean of St. Paul's and at King Charles's court; yet his biographer believed that the signs of his last illness were then growing upon him. The letters probably written about 1628 mentioned a recurrent fever coming on every half year, from which he was used to recover while he could 'eat and digest well enough'. Then in

August 1630 Walton recorded that, while on a visit to one of his daughters,

> he there fell into a fever, which with the help of his constant infirmity (vapors from the spleen) hastened him into so visible a Consumption, that his beholders might say, as to St. Paul of himself, *He dies dayly*.

This sickness, Walton said, continued long, 'weakening and wearying him', and leading ultimately to his death. Later in the year it was even rumoured that he had died, though he was able to write to a friend that,

> the hour of my death, and the day of my buriall, were related in the highest place of this Kingdom. I had at that time no kind of sicknesse, nor was otherwise, then I had been ever since my feavour, and even yet, that is, too weak at this time of the year to go forth, especiallie to London.[1]

In fact, his usual recovery from his recurrent fever had not taken place, and the suspicion arises that some other, more serious, condition had by now taken a hold on him. His weakness without other symptoms increased and by December he felt that it was necessary for him to make his will. He was unable to preach his usual Christmas sermon before the King, but when he received notice to preach at Whitehall on the first Friday in Lent, that is on 12 February 1630/1, he determined to perform this duty and journeyed to London a few days in advance. This determination to proceed in spite of his grave physical condition may have been fortified by a death-wish he had expressed not long before in a letter to a friend:

> It hath been my desire, (and God may be pleased to grant it to me) that I might die in the Pulpit; if not that, yet that I might take my death in the Pulpit, that is, die the sooner by occasion of my former labours.[2]

Arrived in London, he at once consulted his physician, Dr. Simeon Fox, and he, alarmed at his patient's low state, dictated measures 'to

---

[1] Letter to George Garrard, *Tobie Matthew Collection*, 1660, p. 339.
[2] *Letters*, 1651, p. 243.

build up his strength and put some flesh on his bones'. He advised cordials, that is, appetizers, 'and drinking milk twenty days together', but the patient 'passionately denied to drink it'. Walton says that he finally consented to take milk for ten days, but refused to continue another ten days even if it were to add twenty years to his life. The clinical picture was therefore of a man shewing loss of appetite, extreme emaciation, and weakness, though without other obvious symptoms and not suffering loss of mental capacity. This suggests to a professional mind[1] that Donne was in the last stages of a gastric cancer, since this may sometimes creep up gradually and unsuspected on the patient, who does not complain of much pain or other discomforts. The patient does not admit to himself quite how sick he is and will insist on carrying out some important duty. So it was with Donne, who, in spite of his feebleness, forced himself to preach his sermon, though he was delayed for a few days, probably owing to the illness and death of his mother. It was on Friday 25 February that he went to preach at the chapel at Whitehall. According to Walton:

> Many of his friends (who with sorrow saw his sickness had left him onely so much flesh as did onely cover his bones) doubted his strength to perform that task, and, did therefore disswade him from undertaking it, assuring him however, it was like to shorten his life; but, he passionately denied their requests; saying, *he would not doubt that that God who in so many weaknesses had assisted him with an unexpected strength, would now withdraw it in his last employment; professing an holy ambition to perform that sacred work.* And, when to the amazement of some beholders he appeared in the Pulpit, many of them thought he presented himself not to preach mortification by a living voice: but, mortality by a decayed body and dying face. And doubtless, many did secretly ask that question in *Ezekiel; Do these bones live? or, can that soul organize that tongue, to speak so long time as the sand in that glass will move towards its centre, and measure out an hour of this dying mans unspent life?* Doubtless it cannot; and yet, after

[1] This opinion was formed independently. Afterwards I found that the same conclusion had been reached by an eminent physician, Sir Norman Moore, in 1899, his reasons being given in Sir Edmund Gosse's *Life of Donne*, 1899, vol. ii, Appendix E, pp. 373-5.

some faint pauses in his zealous prayer, his strong desires enabled his weak body to discharge his memory of his preconceived meditations, which were of dying, the Text being, *To God the Lord belong the issues from death.* Many that then saw his tears, and heard his faint and hollow voice, professing they thought the Text prophetically chosen, and that *Dr.* Donne *had preach't his own funeral Sermon.*

His sermon preached, his duty done, Donne returned home exhausted and willing to rest. Walton says that he then opened his mind to an unnamed friend, reviewing his life, his time in the ministry, his relations with his family and friends, and the state of his conscience, concluding:

I am to be judged by a merciful God, *who is not willing to see what I have done amiss.* And, though of myself I have nothing to present to him but sins and misery; yet, I know he looks not upon me now as I am of my self, but as I am in my Saviour, and hath given me even at this time some testimonies by his Holy Spirit, that I am of the number of his Elect: *I am therefore full of joy, and shall dye in peace...*

Upon *Monday* following, he took his last leave of his beloved Study; and being sensible of his hourly decay, retired himself to his chamber: and, that week sent at several times for many of his most considerable friends, with whom he took a solemn and deliberate farewell...And now he had nothing to do but to dye; to do which, he stood in need of no longer time, for he had studied long, and to so happy a perfection, that in a former sickness he called God to witness [in his Book of Devotions] *he was that minute ready to deliver his soule into his hands, if that minute God would determine his dissolution...*He lay fifteen dayes earnestly expecting his hourly change; and, in the last hour of his last day, as his body melted away and vapoured into spirit, his soul having, I verily believe, some Revelation of the Beatifical Vision, he said, *I were miserable if I might not dye*; and after those words closed many periods of his faint breath, by saying often, *Thy Kingdom come, Thy Will be done.* His speech, which had long been his ready and faithful servant, left him not till the last minute of his life, and then forsook him; not to serve another Master, but dyed before him; for that it was become useless to him that now conversed with God on earth, as Angels are said to do in heaven, *onely by thoughts and looks*. Being speechless, he did as St. *Stephen, look stedfastly towards heaven, till he saw the Son of God standing at the right hand of his Father*: and being satisfied with this blessed sight, as his soul ascended, and his last breath departed from him, he closed his own eyes; and then, disposed his hands and body into such a posture as required not the least alteration by those that came to shroud him.

Warden Sparrow has concluded from an examination of the circumstances of Donne's life that there was no dramatic moment in his career when he was suddenly converted, no 'single great change making a sanctified out of an unregenerate character'.[1] There was instead a continuous, though quick, development of his sense of mission in his ministry, and there can be no doubt that, when he had become conscious of this, the whole manner of his delivery came to have in it an element of drama. The testimony of the witnesses already quoted suggests this. The often elaborate construction of his sentences and of the periods of his sermons could only have their effect if given with deliberate dramatic intention by their preacher. Every sermon came to be a 'performance', carefully prepared beforehand, committed to memory, and accompanied, it can hardly be doubted, by a voice and gestures like those of an accomplished actor – though it is not intended to imply any insincerity by this comparison.

When Donne prepared his last sermon he was fully aware that he was dying and was more than ever conscious of the drama of the occasion. Walton spoke of 'his tears, his faint and hollow voice', for he was very weak, but this change from his usual vigour, and even passion, would enhance rather than diminish the theatrical value of his situation. That this was deliberate is evident from the extraordinary preparations organized with care by Donne and his physician, Dr. Fox, well in advance of the final scene in the pulpit. Walton has described this episode in a famous passage, which must be quoted *in extenso*:

[1] 'Donne's religious development', *Theology*, xii, 1931, p. 145.

It is observed, that a desire of glory or commendation is rooted in the very nature of man,...which I mention, because Dr. *Donne*, by the persuasion of Dr. *Fox*, easily yielded at this very time to have a Monument made for him; but Dr. *Fox* undertook not to persuade how or what it should be; that was left to Dr. *Donne* himself.

This being resolved upon, Dr. *Donne* sent for a Carver to make for him in wood the figure of an *Urn*, giving him directions for the compass and height of it; and, to bring with it a board of the height of his body. These being got, then without delay a choice Painter was to be in readiness to draw his picture, which was taken as followeth. – Several Charcole-fires being first made in his large Study, he brought with him into that place his winding-sheet in his hand; and, having put off all his cloaths, had this sheet put on him, and so tyed with knots at his head and feet, and his hands so placed, as dead bodies are usually fitted to be shrowded and put into the grave. Upon this *Urn* he thus stood with his eyes shut, and with so much of the sheet turned aside as might shew his lean, pale, and death-like face; which was purposely turned toward the East, from whence he expected the second coming of his and our Saviour. Thus he was drawn at his just height; and when the picture was fully finished, he caused it to be set by his bed-side, where it continued, and became his hourly object till his death: and, was then given to his dearest friend and Executor Dr. *King*, who caused him to be thus carved in one entire piece of white Marble, as it now stands in the Cathedral Church of St. *Pauls*; and by Dr. *Donne's* own appointment, these words were to be affixed to it as his Epitaph:

JOHANNES DONNE
Sac. Theol. Professor
Post varia Studia quibus ab annis tenerrimus
fideliter, nec infeliciter incubuit;
Instinctu & impulsu Sp. Sancti, Monitu
& Hortatu
REGIS JACOBI, Ordines Sacros amplexus
Anno sui Jesu, 1614. & suæ ætatis 42.

PLATE 2

Decanatu hujus Ecclesiæ indutus 27. Novem-
bris. 1621.
Exutus morte ultimo Die Martii 1631
Hic licet in Occiduo Cinere Aspicit Eum
Cujus nomen est Oriens.

Above the entablature carrying this epitaph was an armorial shield, supported by swags, impaling the arms of Donne with those of the Cathedral.

AS recorded in his Epitaph, Donne had died on 31 March 1631. He was buried on 3 April in a position in the Cathedral designated by himself some years before, so that he might see his last resting place twice daily as he passed by to perform his public duties as Dean. According to Walton, Donne had wished to be buried privately, but many friends, who had known and honoured him, wished to shew their feelings 'by a voluntary and sad attendance of his body to the grave', where flowers were scattered for several days until the masons had sealed the stones. Sir Lucius Cary in his 'elegy on Dr. Donne' exclaimed:

> Let Laud his funerall Sermon preach, and shew
> Those vertues, dull eyes were not apt to know,

though in fact there is no evidence that the Archbishop or any other person preached at the funeral.

Soon afterwards Henry King was sent an anonymous gift of 100 marks towards the cost of making an effigy commissioned from Nicholas Stone, one of the foremost monumental masons of the time. It was only after the death of Dr. Fox in 1642 that he became known as the donor. Stone recorded in his notebook that he was paid £120 for doing the work, giving £8 to another mason, Humphrey Mayer, who finished it. The statue in Italian marble was provided with an entablature at the top carrying the Epitaph. It has often been noticed that the folds of the linen shrouding the body suggest that the figure was recumbent, not standing, though the feet are resting on the urn as if to proclaim ultimate resurrection. It is surmised that the sculptor could not conceive

41

of the figure having been in any other position than recumbent, whatever the drawing seemed to indicate. The face was thought to be so good a likeness that Sir Henry Wotton was reported by Walton to have said that 'it seems to breathe faintly; and Posterity shall look upon it as a kind of artificial Miracle'.

Engravings of the effigy were included in Henry Holland's *Ecclesia Sancti Pauli Illustrata*, London, 1633, and in miniature in the engraved title-pages of the fourth and fifth editions of Donne's *Devotions*, 1634 and 1638. It was also pictured as a large engraving by Hollar in Dugdale's *History of St. Paul's Cathedral*, London, 1658, with an inscription in a cartouche alongside recording that it had already suffered injury by impious hands, but was restored by the care of Margaret and Christopher Clapham of Bramesley in Yorkshire (plate 2). When the Cathedral was destroyed by fire in 1666, Donne's monument was almost the only one to be saved intact. Inevitably it was dismantled, and during the rebuilding by Sir Christopher Wren was stored with the mutilated fragments of other monuments in the crypt. There it remained throughout the eighteenth century and into the nineteenth. Dr. Gough, the antiquary, described[1] what he found on 19 May 1783 in the part of the crypt dedicated to St. Faith the Virgin. He saw a number of figures mutilated, though in a tolerable state of preservation, among them Donne's entire figure:

> The urn, flat at top and never open, in the window of a separate vault, and fragments of his tomb are on the opposite side of the church...at the feet of Dr. Donne's statue being fragments of monuments, pieces of pillars, arms, pedestals and dust. Below the window, on the floor, the urn belonging to the Doctor's figure, and a heap of rubbish intermixed with various bones thrown from graves at different periods.

John Peller Malcolm visited the place twenty years later and described very much the same state of affairs. In his book, *Londinium Redivivum*, London, 1803, vol. III, is an engraving of the scene, shewing Donne's effigy propped against a wall surrounded by other miscellaneous fragments (plate 3). At length, about the year 1818, the portions of the

---

[1] Richard Gough, *Sepulchral Monuments of Great Britain*, Part II, 1796, p. cccxxiv.

PLATE 3

monument were re-assembled and placed where it may be seen today, in the south aisle of the choir, as near as may be to its original position in the old Cathedral. A photograph taken recently by permission of the Very Reverend Martin Sullivan, Dean of St. Paul's, is reproduced here (plate 4). The entablature and the arms above it are not included in the reproduction. When these are compared with their representation in the engraving given by Dugdale in his *History of St. Paul's*, it can be seen that there are many differences in detail. It seems probable that, when the monument was re-assembled, this portion was missing or badly damaged, and that the present sculpture is a replica made to replace the original stone.

The painting on a board served not only as a guide for the sculptor, but was also the source of the engraving of Donne's head in his shroud prefixed to his last sermon when it was printed in 1632. This image (plate 1) conveys even more faithfully than does the effigy, his 'lean, pale and death-like face' described by Walton. The engraving was executed by Martin Droeshout, a Fleming working in England from 1620 to 1651. He had engraved, among many others, the head of Shakespeare used as frontispiece in the folio edition of the plays in 1623. The oval surrounding Donne's head bears the legend:

EFFIGIES REVERENDISS: UIRI IOHANNIS DONNE
NUPER ECCLES: PAULINAE DECANI.

Below it is the inscription:

Corporis hæc Animæ sit Syndon Syndon Jesu. Amen.

Dame Helen Gardner, Professor of English Literature in the University of Oxford, has pointed out that this Latin hexameter presents some difficulty in both sense and scansion. She interprets the meaning as being:

May this shroud of the body be the shroud of the soul:
the shroud of Jesus.

and believes that it was composed by Donne himself. Warden Sparrow[1] suggests as an alternative that the words composed by Donne were

[1] *Times Literary Supplement*, 13 March 1953, p. 169.

43

transposed by him or by a puzzled copyist in order to improve the scansion, the correct order being:

Corporis hæc Syndon, Syndon animæ sit Jesu,

that is,

This is my body's shroud, may my soul's shroud be that of Jesus.

He adds that Donne was certainly familiar with Alfonso Paleoti's treatise[1] on the Sindon, or winding-sheet, of Christ preserved at Turin, and suggests further that a play upon the words, 'John Donne, sin done', may have been in Donne's mind.

Soon after preaching his last sermon Donne had been visited by his friend and executor, Henry King, and had delivered into his hands the sermon notes and other manuscripts as already mentioned. There can be no doubt that at the same time he gave King the manuscript of his sermon with instructions to have it printed. This he may have had by him in the pulpit lest his weakness should impair his ability to speak from memory. It is evident that, for unknown reasons, King was slow to act; when he did send the script to the printer he added two 'Elegies' on the author, one, the longer, was by himself; the other, called 'An Epitaph on Dr. Donne', was anonymous, but was signed 'Edw. Hyde' when it was reprinted in the first edition of Donne's *Poems*, 1633, p. 377. This signatory has been thought to be the Rev. Edward Hide, a royalist clergyman, who was educated at Westminster School and Cambridge and wrote various tracts, sermons and Latin poems. More probably, however, he was Sir Edward Hyde, afterwards Lord Chancellor Clarendon, this identification having been made in a copy of Donne's *Poems*, 1639, by Giles Oldisworth, another royalist divine, who was a contemporary of Abraham Cowley at Westminster School and Cambridge and a careful student of Donne's poems.[2]

---

[1] *Iesu Christi Crucifixi Stigmata Sacræ Sindoni impressa*, folio, Venice, 1620.

[2] Oldisworth's book was described in detail by the late Dr. John Sampson of Liverpool University in *Essays and Studies by Members of The English Association*, vol. VII, Oxford, 1921, pp. 82–107. The book was afterwards given to me by Dr. Sampson and is still in my library, where is also a manuscript collection of Donne's poems carrying at each end the signature 'Edward Hyde', These have been identfied as Clarendon's, when a young man, by comparison with others in documents in Oxford (Bodleian Library and University Archives).

PLATE 4

The thin quarto volume containing Donne's sermon was not entered at Stationers' Hall until 30 September 1631, five months after Donne's death, under the hands of two Wardens of the Company and of Thomas Buckner, Chaplain to the Archbishop of Canterbury. When it was registered the book was not given any title, though when printed the title-page carried the words:

> *Deaths Duell, or, A Consolation to the Soule, against the*
> *dying Life, and living Death of the Body,*

with the further explanation,

> *Being his last Sermon, and called by His Majesties houshold*
> THE DOCTORS OWNE FUNERALL SERMON.

It was formerly assumed that this wording was composed by the publishers, Richard Redmer and Benjamin Fisher, whose names appear in the imprint of the first edition. Recently Dame Helen Gardner has made the interesting suggestion that the wording of the title had been formulated by Donne himself and that he had arranged for the engraving of his shrouded head to be placed opposite this arresting form of words. The theory is attractive and the whole plan would have been in character, carrying to a conclusion the self-conscious drama of the author's death. It would be wrong, however, to ignore the fact that another claim has been made. It is known that the two key words, DEATHS DUELL, had been already used as the title of another book entered at Stationers' Hall for William Stansby more than three months earlier. This was under the date 15 June 1631, the book being Walter Coleman's undistinguished poems afterwards published with the title:

> *La Dance Machabre or Deaths Duell by W. C.*
> *London Printed by William Stansby.*

The actual date of its publication is not known, but it must have been later than the appearance of Donne's sermon, since Coleman added after his poems the following lines of doggerel:

> The Authors Apologie for the title of his Booke
> iniuriously conferd by Roger Muchill, upon a
> Sermon of Doctor Donnes.

Death in a furie hath the Fellon tooke
That stole my Title, *Donne*, to grace thy booke.
To wrong the liuing and commit a rape
Vpon the dead, how could he thinke to scape?
I am but too much honord to be stil'd
Th'vnwilling Gossip to thy vnknowne child.
But he that sought so basely my disgrace
Behind my backe: hath wrong'd thee to thy face.
I would reuenge thy quarrell but that he
That deales with dirt shall but defiled be.
Liue in thy liuing fame; and let this serue
Not thine, but mine owne honor to preserue.

An Epitaph vpon Roger
Muchill

Here lies Much-ill *that here did good* (*who thought*
To coozen Death) *in his untimely vault.*
Harme watch, harme catch, his auarice was such
That at the length, he stole a Pot to much.
But he that would not take his bond before
May take his word, he shall doe so no more.

Walter Coleman, or Colman, belonged to a Roman Catholic family from Staffordshire and was educated at the English College at Douai in Flanders, doing further study in France. Later he entered the convent of the English Franciscans of the Strict Observance, and after being ordained priest was sent to the mission in England. He was arrested on arrival and subjected to ridicule because, according to the rules of his order, he wore no shirt. He was imprisoned for refusing to take the oath of allegiance, but was released through the influence of friends and was able to serve the mission for several years until he was again arrested and imprisoned at the Old Bailey. He was tried with six other priests in December 1641 and was condemned to death, but was repeatedly reprieved by Charles I, ultimately dying a lingering death in Newgate Prison in 1645.[1] *Deaths Duell*, dedicated in French to the

[1] *Dictionary of National Biography*, vol. XI, 1887.

LA DANCE
MACHABRE
or
Deaths Duell
by
W. C.
LONDON
Printed by William
Stansby.

PLATE 5

Queen, is his only publication. It is a very uncommon book[1] with an engraved title-page by Thomas Cecill (plate 5), in which the book-title is surrounded by an allegorical design with the figures of Time and Death.

It was natural to suggest that perhaps Redmer was responsible for the title, for he seemed to have had a particular interest in Donne's *Deaths Duell*, having inserted in one copy a specially printed leaf with a dedicatory letter addressed *To his dearest sister Mrs Elizabeth Francis of Brumstead in Norff*. Coleman's claim now implies that the title, *Deaths Duell*, was not the invention of Donne or his publisher, but had been plagiarized in the first place by Roger Mitchell, a bookseller operating in partnership with Michael Sparke at the Bull's Head in St. Paul's Churchyard from 1627 until his death in 1631.[2] Mitchell, lampooned by Coleman as Roger Much-ill, was not previously known to have had any connexion with Donne's sermon, and it seems odd that this relatively obscure publisher should have been privileged to handle such a literary prize. It seems that after Mitchell's death in 1631 the rights were transferred to Redmer and Fisher and his name passed out of the story.

D EATHS DUELL, published in 1632 and printed, it is assumed, under the eye of Dr. Henry King, forms a very thin quarto volume. It has an elaborate title-page (reproduced on p. 48) faced by Droeshout's macabre engraving. The brief Preface is signed R., as if written by the publisher, Richard Redmer, but the words, if not actually composed by Walton, bear the unmistakable stamp of his influence.

[1] Coleman's connexion with Donne was first noticed by Frank B. Williams of Harvard University, and the book was described by me in the *Times Literary Supplement*, 24 September 1938. Six copies of *La Dance Machabre* are known, in the Bodleian Library, Oxford; the Dyce Collection, Victoria and Albert Museum; the British Museum; Harvard University Library; the Huntington Library, California, and the Britwell Court Library, the portion sold at Sotheby's, 29 March 1971, lot. 104.
[2] *Dictionary of Booksellers and Printers 1557–1640*, Bibliographical Society, London, 1910, pp. 191–2.

DEATHS
DVELL,
O R,

A Consolation to the Soule, against
the dying Life, and liuing
Death of the Body.

Deliueredin a Sermon at White Hall, before the
KINGS MAIESTY, *in the beginning*
of Lent, 1630.

By that late learned and Reuerend Diuine,
IOHN DONNE, Dr. in Diuinity,
& Deane of S.*Pauls*, London.
Being his last Sermon, and called by his Maiesties houshold
THE DOCTORS OWNE FVNERALL SERMON:

LONDON,
Printed by THOMAS HARPER, for *Richard Redmer*
and *Beniamin Fisher*, and are to be sold at the signe
of the Talbot in Alders-gate street.
M.DC.XXXII.

TO THE READER

This Sermon was by Sacred Authority, stiled the Authors own Funerall Sermon. Most fitly: whether we respect the time or the matter. It was preached not many dayes before his death; as if, having done this, there remained nothing for him to do, but to dye: And the matter is, of Death; the occasion and subject of all Funerall Sermons. It hath beene observed of this Reverend Man, That his faculty in Preaching continually incı eased: and, That as he exceeded others at first; so at last he exceeded himselfe. This is the last Sermon; I will not say, it is therefore his best; because all his were excellent. Yet thus much: A dying Mans words, if they concerne ourselves; doe usually make the deepest impression, as being spoken most feelingly, and with least affectation. Now whom doth it concerne to learne, both the danger, and benefit of death? Death is every mans Enemy, and intends hurt to all, though to many, he be the occasion of greatest good. This Enemy we must all combat dying; whom he living did almost conquer, having discovered the utmost of his power, the utmost of his cruelty. May we make such use of this and other the like preparatives, That neither death, whensoever it shall come may seeme terrible, nor life tedious, how long soever it shall last.

R.

Donne took his text from *Psalms*, lxviii, verse 20:

And unto God, the Lord, belong the issues from Death,

altering 'from Death' to 'of Death'.

He opened his discourse by likening God to a building with its foundations, buttresses and 'contignations that knit and unite them'. God, owning all the issues of death, is the God of salvations and in this capacity controls the three main issues – *a morte, in morte, per mortem*. The three parts, into which the sermon thus naturally falls, deal in turn with the three issues – life, death and the consequences of death. The first part, *a morte*, is very much longer than the other two. In the printed text the beginning of each part is marked in the margin, and in the present edition by the use of a large initial letter.

In the first part the *exitus mortis* is regarded as a liberation *by* death, every previous event of our life having been 'so many passages from death to death'. Even birth is an issue from the 'death' in our mother's womb, this idea being elaborated in a series of extensions in many directions, including a consideration of Eve's giving birth to Cain as an example of the body's being but the house of death. Yet this *exitus a morte* is only an entry into another death, death by imprisonment in a body destined for the grave. Man's pilgrimage through life is pictured as a varied sequence of deaths, illustrated by numerous examples from the scriptures. In a crescendo of eloquence the preacher rivets attention on the horrors of mortality and corruption, common to all men with the single exception of Christ, everything being the purpose and will of God. The mystery of Christ's incorruptibility is shewn as an earnest of ultimate human participation, in spite of the second posthumous death by decay and vermiculation. Even death by incineration is defeated by the God who is able to re-inanimate the recompacted dust. All these deaths are the purposes of God leading to ultimate deliverance.

In the second part the preacher announces that among the issues of death, when it comes, is God's right to pass a judgement upon us. Physicians have rules for their prognostications, but we have no means from what we see of death for knowing in advance of spiritual death and damnation. Man hates to die and God does not promise an easy death, but whether the gate of his prison is opened 'with an oyled key' or is hewn down with violence, a gate there will be, and the soul is God's care.

The third part elaborates the idea of liberation *per mortem*, that is, liberation from death through the death of another, the death of Christ. In a series of tremendous passages Christ's death is described, explained and justified, leading to the final abandonment of the preacher's humbled audience hanging upon him that hangs upon the Cross, awaiting their reward bought 'with the inestimable price of his incorruptible blood'.

Donne's vocabulary and manipulation of words are well illustrated in this sermon. Like a later writer, Sir Thomas Browne, he was addicted to the use of long words, usually of classical derivation. In this sermon we find: *colluctations, cribration, hypostatical, nullification, perigrination, presagitions, recompacting, re-inanimation, verisimulated, vermiculation, vilification*, and many others. He even invented at least one new word, used in his first paragraph:

contignation (a position close to),

which has not been noted by the lexicographers. If the whole body of sermons were to be searched, others would no doubt be found. An unusual compound word is *death-turfe*, for a hermit's death-bed. Having found the words that pleased him, he was much given to repeating them once or twice in a line or two further on, sometimes accompanied by other words with the same meaning, such as:

this obligation, this Oportuit, *this necessity.*

Donne knew how to use all the turns and tricks of rhetoric to best advantage. In this, his last, 'his own funeral', sermon, he had the art and the presence by which to involve his audience in the agonies of his own impending dissolution, tempered, for their comfort, by his faith in a merciful God.

WE have no knowledge of how many copies of a book such as *Deaths Duell* are likely to have been printed; the only indications are that it is very uncommon today, and that a second edition was called for in the following year, both facts pointing to the conclusion that the edition of 1632 was small. In 1633 it was even smaller, this edition being scarcer than the first. The same engraved plate was used for the frontispiece in both, and the prints reveal no sign of wear, as if the plate had not been required to yield a large number of impressions. The texts in the first two editions have only a few minor differences, but when the sermon was reprinted in the third folio volume of 1660 a great many changes were introduced, and it is apparent that Henry King in 1632 and the younger Donne in 1660 were using different manuscripts. The variations have been listed by the late George Potter and Evelyn Simpson in their tenth volume of the *Collected Sermons*, published by the University of California Press in the years 1953 to 1956. These editors found that the later text was in many respects better than the earlier one, though they chose to print

51

this through feeling that King's manuscript was closer to the author. Donne had lived long enough after preaching his sermon to have the opportunity of making some revision, though it is very unlikely that, in his enfeebled state, he would have copied it out himself. He may thus have directed some verbal changes, but most of the variations were certainly not his, being seen in modernized spelling and punctuation. These must have been made by a copyist, probably the younger Donne, who also greatly reduced the number of words to be printed in italic. In 1632 a few words had been accidentally omitted by the printer, but these would have been restored in any reprint.

As Potter and Simpson observed, the modernized version is easier to read today. This simplification is important, the sequence of words being already in themselves hard enough to follow. The sentences are composed with deliberate art in such a way as to sharpen the attention of audience or reader. They seem to vibrate in several directions at once, so that the meaning is constantly and unexpectedly changing course. The excessive amount of italic type (fashionable in 1632), or, in the manuscript, underlining, may have had some significance for the writer when he put it on paper, such as determining emphasis by voice or gesture, but to modern readers it is slightly confusing. In the later version, chosen for the present reprint, italic is used almost only for quotations, Latin words, and proper names.

In addition, for the present text, the whole has been critically examined in the light of the variations in the two texts listed by Potter and Simpson (*Sermons*, vol. x, pp. 278–92) and those readings, which seem to me to be the best, have been adopted throughout; while following the folio in the main, this reprint should thus present the best form that can be attained. Some obvious misprints have been corrected.

GEOFFREY KEYNES

Readings in Deaths Duell *taken from the quarto of
1632 in preference to those of the folio of 1660*

PRINTED AND BOUND
IN CAMBRIDGE AT THE
UNIVERSITY PRINTING HOUSE
(BROOKE CRUTCHLEY, UNIVERSITY PRINTER)

THE PAPER MADE UNDER THE SUPERVISION
OF THE HALE PAPER COMPANY
THE WATERMARK DESIGNED
BY BRAM DE DOES